BE THOU ENCOURAGED

BE THOU ENCOURAGED

Forty Poems of Faith

JONATHAN CORDERO

RESOURCE *Publications* · Eugene, Oregon

BE THOU ENCOURAGED
Forty Poems of Faith

Resource Publications
An Imprint of Wipf and Stock Publishers
199 W. 8th Ave., Suite 3
Eugene, OR 97401

www.wipfandstock.com

PAPERBACK ISBN: 978-1-6667-4259-6
HARDCOVER ISBN: 978-1-6667-4260-2
EBOOK ISBN: 978-1-6667-4261-9

MAY 27, 2022 1:56 PM

Dedicated to Ruth and Anthony,
My angels looking down

Contents

Introduction | ix

Anointed, Sanctified, and Hallowed | 3

I Shall Want for Nothing | 4

Thou Shalt See It Come to Pass | 5

All That I Have Is Thine | 6

O Merciful God | 7

Everlasting Mercy | 8

Created to Praise Thee | 9

A Poem for the Morning | 10

He Rescued Me | 11

Suffer Me to Speak | 12

They Lie in Wait | 15

An Husband Unto Me | 16

True Riches | 17

Desire Understanding | 18

Exceeding Great Reward | 19

The Death of Former Things | 20

Thou Art My Rest | 21

Be Thou Moved by the Spirit | 22

His Temple | 23

Who Am I? | 24

A Poem for Communion | 27

Sing Unto the Lord | 28

A Poem of Repentance | 29

Breaches in Mine Armour | 30

Fall Short in Comparison | 31

Similitudes | 32

The Beauty of the Lord | 33

Thy Righteousness Shall Abide | 34

Rebuke the Thick Cloud | 35

A Poem of Healing | 36

He Shall Gather | 39

We Thy People | 40

Thy Church | 41

Praise with Thy Entire Being | 42

Prayer of the Youthful Servant | 43

Be Thou with Me | 44

Love Even Thine Enemies | 45

Get Thee Behind Me, O Satan | 46

All Things Are Possible for God | 47

Faith | 48

Introduction

G od is worthy to be praised with every gift and talent that we possess. This I've known since my youth, but I have not always paired this knowledge with action. Since my formative years in grade school, I've always loved poetry and creative writing as a whole. I've used this gift in many different ways over the years. Some of my first memories consist of me writing poetry on loose-leaf binder paper and then seeing them hung on the bulletin board outside of my classroom. When I was eleven years old, I was inspired by the works of Tolkien to write a short fantasy novel. Three years later, I recomposed that same novel into a two-hundred-page manuscript with the newfound knowledge that I had acquired from my time in middle school. I later got into songwriting and screenwriting, but none of my efforts to use my gift ever came to much beyond the writings residing permanently in either a drawer or a hard drive. The lack of success that I had seen in all of my ventures into creative writing left me not only discouraged but I was also left uncertain if this was even a gift that I truly possessed. It wasn't until years later when my love for Christ had been rekindled, and when I found myself with a deep yearning to be used by Him that I realized that my gift was not meant to be used to entertain or to conform to the world, but rather, my gift was meant to be used to glorify God and to push forward the gospel of the Kingdom.

As with the understanding of His word, I feel that God eased me into the process of writing this book of poetry. I began writing my first Christian poems when I'd wake up suddenly in the middle of the night to pray after having been awoken by terrible nightmares and cold sweats. While the attacks of the enemy were strong enough to wake me, God's Spirit was stronger in that He kept me awake and moved me to write expressions of love and gratitude towards Him. I later began to willingly wake up in the early hours of the morning simply to give Him glory with the fruit of my lips, and simply to give Him honor with my fingers by writing poems of faith. Soon, the empty pages of my small journal began to fill, and at the recommendation of a friend, I decided that I would put an effort into writing a formal book of poems with the purpose of encouraging and edifying the reader while praising God simultaneously.

Out of the many inspirations behind this book, the chief of them all is the biblical book of Psalms. While the Hebrew Psalms do rhyme on occasion, the rhetorical device used far more frequently is parallelism. The Psalmists often juxtapose the righteous with the wicked, daytime with night, the strength of God with the weakness of men, and many other polar opposites for the purpose of illustrating visceral messages to the audience. Being that I've turned to these sacred writings for encouragement throughout many of my days as a Christian, it was natural that when I decided to take pen in hand and write my own odes to the Lord, I mimicked the writing style of the aforementioned authors. While my act of imitation initially started unintentionally with small allusions to the Psalms sprinkled throughout my early poems, I soon realized that I enjoyed referencing these sacred texts as a source of inspiration for my own writings. Many of the poems included in this book are very much unabashed reworkings of the material found throughout the book of Psalms. For this reason, I chose to forgo the usage of rhymes, and instead fully immersed myself in parallelism with the purpose of using it as the primary rhetorical device in this book.

Another unique feature of *Be Thou Encouraged* is the usage of Early Modern English instead of standard twenty-first century English vernacular. This too started unintentionally due to the fact that the Bible translation that I've read since my youth is the King James Version. What started as a sporadic inclusion of "Thou" when addressing the Lord directly later became a full-on project incorporating an archaic version of English. While some may view this feature as cumbersome or perhaps even redundant, I find that this antiquated version of the English language carries a force and beauty that is simply unmatched by modern vernacular. There is a timeless eloquence possessed by the Authorized Version of the Bible, the writings of John Milton, and many other classic English Christian texts that I desired to emulate in this book. I also implemented this form of English due to the fact that earlier versions of the language possess some features that modern English lacks, such as having both singular and plural second-person pronouns. I've put a painstaking effort into learning this version of the language and all of its intricacies including its grammar, spelling, and overall syntax. While much subtlety was put into the writing and editing of this book, I realize that there may be minor miscues in overall consistency that I have possibly overlooked due to the fact that this version of English is rather obscure. My hope is that the reader would view this writing feature as a quaint addition to the book rather than a superfluous idiosyncrasy.

Life is not easy: especially for a Christian. We all know that different trials arise daily, but we must always remember to not only be encouraged when we are in a season of plenty, for we must also remain encouraged when a season of drought is brought upon us to strengthen our faith. When I began writing the contents of this book, I used many of my life experiences as inspiration for the themes presented in the poems. I learned that my wife was pregnant with our first child when I was still in the early stages of working on this book. The joy of that news added a whole new perspective and motivation to complete the project that I had begun just a few months prior. I knew that if my writings were never read by anyone else, they would at least be read by my child. With that in mind, I wrote of the mishaps and mistakes that I had made throughout my adolescence and young adulthood. I also wrote of the many times that I had felt depleted and defeated, and the many times that God had lifted me back on my feet again. I hoped that when my child was old enough, they'd read this book that their father wrote and find some encouragement in it. But as I continued to work, it seemed that the closer I got to completion, the more the enemy placed hurdles in my path to stop me from achieving my goal. We lost our firstborn child when my wife was thirty-three weeks pregnant; I had just finished what I thought would be the final round of revisions earlier that same week. The pain that we felt at that time and even now cannot be explained in speech or in writing. I shelved the project the day that we lost our child. I couldn't imagine releasing a book written with the purpose of encouraging others when I had just been utterly defeated. It wasn't until a year later that God gave me the strength to resume my work again. Despite that horrible event that occurred in my life, I can honestly say that the Lord never left my side at any point. I know firsthand that He is a lifter of the downtrodden and a healer of the weak and broken-hearted. It is my sincere and earnest desire that the reader would find encouragement in these poems. It is also my hope that this book would be a source of strength whenever the reader finds their faith weakened. Above all, I hope that God is glorified in every word written.

"Before I formed thee in the belly I knew thee;
and before thou camest forth out of the womb
I sanctified thee"

꧁꧂

JEREMIAH 1:5 KJV

Anointed, Sanctified, and Hallowed

The Lord doth not abide in the congregation of the wicked; neither doth the Almighty dwell within the body of him that is unclean. O Lord, what must men do, that they might receive Thy Holy Spirit? Surely they must believe that He is, and surely they must be washed of their sins. Selah. Pour Thy oil upon my head, O Lord: may Thy ointment run down as waters upon the crown of my head, that it might fall unto my beard, and even unto my garment. Sanctify all that I am, to the end that I might be holy unto Thee, O God. As all the vessels and that which was within the tabernacle were anointed and hallowed, and as Aaron and his sons were washed and sanctified, do Thou even unto me. For my soul and my body are possessions of Thine; my life and my death are in the hands of the Almighty. O Lord, even if my body doth go down to the dust from which it was taken, spare my soul and bring it unto Thee. O Lord, if my portion is to die by the sword of wicked transgressors, it is Thy hands which I have fallen into and not the hands of mine enemies. For the sparrows fall not without Thou giving Thy consent, and the leaves wither not without Thou giving Thy command. Therefore if I fall, it is to the end that I might be raised again. Therefore if I die, it is to the end that I might glorify my Father.

I Shall Want for Nothing

Why should I fear? Or why should I worry? My God made the heavens and the earth. Will I ever lack bread, or feel the chill of an uncovered back? Surely I shall want for nothing, if I have hope in the Lord. For He shall grant me the gift of longevity; yea, even everlasting life shall He grant me, for Jesus Christ is my hope and my salvation. If my pillow were a stone, or if my roof were the stars, surely He would comfort me still. If my wife were to leave the husband of her youth, or if my children were to forsake the tree that begat them, I know that my God would sustain me and remain at my side. For when hath the God of heaven and earth ever forsaken me? Or when hath the God of hosts ever failed me? Therefore I know that He shall strengthen the joints of my hands, and cause all my works to prosper. Wisdom shall He also give unto me liberally: therefore shall I speak of his promises unto every man with ears. Wait on the Lord: wait and see the reward that He hath in store for all His saints. For who can imagine the abundance of His goodness? Who can perceive the riches of the Lord? Keep me, O Lord; keep me in Thy word and in Thy truth for all my days. For I earnestly desire to see Thy coming, O God. My soul doth greatly long to be with Thee for evermore.

Thou Shalt See It Come to Pass

Blessed art Thou, O Holy One of Israel! Blessed be the Name of the Lord! Of Him have I received my necessary food; of Him have I received that which is needful for the body. O Lord, it is Thou Who hast made the sheep from which I received wool for my raiment. O Lord, it is Thou Who hast given rain unto my crops. Thou hast caused Thy sun to shine upon my fruit trees. Thou hast also given me favour in the sight of the men that bought of my wares and of my victuals. Through the wisdom that Thou hast put within me, I have had good success in all my doings. Thou hast even given me the desires of my heart which only Thou knewest of. Selah. What reason have I to doubt the assuredness of Thy word? Which of the prophecies in the book of the Lord hath lacked her mate? Hath there ever been a word that proceeded from the mouth of the Lord that hath failed to come to pass? Or will the Lord break the oath which He sware by Himself unto our fathers? God forbid that I should doubt the rock of my salvation; God forbid that I should waver in my faith. For in due season, the Lord shall grant that which He hath been besought for. Thou shalt see it come to pass because thou hast put thy trust in Him.

All That I Have Is Thine

O Lord, O my God, my praises belong unto Thee. My adoration and my devotion belong unto Thee alone. All that I have and all that I am belong unto Thy holy Name. For all the earth is Thine, and all the heavens and that which is within the heavens are Thine. Though I be a caretaker of a vineyard, and though I build me a house to preside over, was not that house built with that which cometh from the earth that the Lord hath created? How can I rebuke the birds that build their nests in the trees of my field? Or how can I cast out the roebuck and the hart that seek to graze upon my pasture? God forbid that I should make clean riddance of my bushes or of my crops. Can I be justified in hiding my face from my brother during his time of need? If I say that he hath no place in my home, or if I say that he cannot be clothed by the wool of my sheep, how then can I stand before my God on the day when I am judged? For God giveth to whom He will according to His purpose; and God taketh from them that rob Him of His glory. O Lord, I am mindful of Thy blessings. O Lord, do that which seemeth right unto Thee concerning me. O Lord, do that which seemeth right unto Thee with all that belongeth unto me.

O Merciful God

O Lord, Thou rebukest men to the end that they might repent. Thou searchest the thoughts and the intents of the mind. Thou dost thoroughly examine our hearts, that Thou mayest reveal unto us our flaws. For a proud look and a risen chin are an abomination in the sight of God. A boastful thought, though it be unspoken, is detestable in the eyes of the Lord. For how long can a man have evil in his heart before he speaketh evil? How long can a man think upon adultery before he committeth the wicked transgression? Nothing is hidden from the Creator of the hiding place: for how can I hide in the forest that He planted? Though I sail to the midst of the sea to seek out a private place, shall not He that poured out the waters find me there? Though my sin be hidden within the depth of my mind, I know that the Lord will shine the light and make it known. For there is nothing hidden, that shall not be revealed; and since I have received knowledge of my sin, what profit shall I have, if I continue to pleasure myself with death? For this cause do I thank thee, O merciful God: for Thou hast exposed the leaven in my heart, that it might be removed. Thou hast put me within the fiery furnace, that I might be refined. Thou hast rebuked me to the end that I might repent; and through Thy chastening, I have seen that Thou art truly a merciful God.

Everlasting Mercy

Daily, O Lord, daily are Thy mercies new unto the children of men. Thy gentleness and lovingkindness have endured from days of old; even from everlasting hath Thy mercy been exemplified. When the thoughts of the hearts of men were only evil continually, Thou didst open the windows of heaven. Thou didst cause all that had the breath of life in their nostrils to perish, but Noah found grace in Thy sight. O how excellent is Thy mercy! For though Thou couldest have wiped the remembrance of Adam from off the face of the earth, Thou didst leave him Shem, Ham and Japheth to replenish the land. Thou didst put fear and dread into the heart of every beast, every fowl, and every fish, that they might submit themselves unto the sons of Noah. O how excellent is Thy mercy! Even when the great rain falleth upon the earth, Thy bow doth appear with glory in the cloud, that Thou mayest remember Thy everlasting covenant. O how excellent is Thy mercy!

CREATED TO PRAISE THEE

O Lord, how excellent is the praise that Thou hast put within every creature, that they might worship Thee. For even the trees, and those tallest amongst them, do lift their limbs in exaltation of Thee. Even the birds offer sacrifices of praise every morning with the sound of their singing. The waters of the sea jump up and down at the thought of Thy majesty. Even if they be still, is it not to shew forth that Thou art the Prince of Peace? The thunders shout mightily in fear of Thy voice. The sun doth bow down in worship and in submission to Thy commandment every evening. The winds cause all nature to dance in every direction, that the praise of the Lord might be shewed forth on earth. The lion roareth in thanksgiving; yea, he crieth joyfully for the provision which Thou hast graciously given unto him. The lamb doth willingly offer himself as a sacrifice unto the God that hath given him life. Selah. Though I have no harp, I will sing unto Thee with my voice. Though I have no drum, I will clap my hands and stomp my feet in a rhythm of praise unto the God of glory. Though my body is weak and filled with infirmities, I will dance as a child danceth. For all things were created to praise Thee: therefore I will be one with creation in my adoration of the mighty God.

A Poem for the Morning

I will give thanks unto my God in the morning. I will arise from my bed and acknowledge the protection that He bestowed upon me as I slept. I will worship the most High God with song and dance for the breath of life that He hath kept in my body. I will glorify the Lord in whatsoever I do, for He hath provided me with all my needs. Selah. As I slept, mine enemies said amongst themselves that I would not rise again. As I slept, they sought to defame my character as one that had not the means to answer them back. As I slept, I glorified my God. He hath maintained my dignity, and He shall recompense all those that wish to curse me. I love the Lord, for He hath lifted me up from a sure death. Which of His foes shall not be put under His feet? I will sing unto the Lord, for He hath rescued me.

He Rescued Me

O Lord, Thy Name alone is life. I called unto Thee and Thou didst hear me from the midst of Thy throne. I cried with a loud voice; yea, I spared not my throat. For an unclean spirit sought to force itself within me, but my God found me in the open field and rescued me. I will not suffer anger nor deceit to have place within my heart, for my reins are searched continuously by the Almighty. How can an unclean spirit dwell in unity with the hidden Man of the heart? For He is a strong Man that cannot be bound; neither doth He suffer the unclean to enter His temple. Selah. I will move about decently for all my days. I will give no reason for accusation to be raised against me by man or by devil. I will recompense evil with good; yea, I will pray for mine enemies and give place unto wrath. For what good doth it serve to store up resentment for my brother? For if I curse him which is made in the likeness and image of God, how then can I bless my Father which is in heaven with the same tongue? Nay, this is folly that cometh from the pit. Rather, I will trust in the Lord Who doth see every man's works and judgeth him justly. I will forgive my brother's transgressions, for the Lord hath forgiven mine. I will bless my neighbour though he sought to curse me. I will be perfect; as the Lord my God is, so shall I be.

Suffer Me to Speak

O Lord, suffer me to speak; grant me the liberty to make my request known unto Thee. For I ask not much, seeing that Thou hast already given me far above mine expectation. Yea, I ask of Thee that which is a light thing in Thy sight. Lord, I supplicate unto Thee that Thou wouldest not suffer me to be deceived by that which vain men that go down to the pit be enamoured with. Again, I ask of Thee that Thou wouldest not suffer me to be deceived by the flattery of an harlot. O Lord, let not a looking glass be a stumblingblock unto me; let not pride nor haughtiness dwell in my reins. Rather, O God, cause Thou me to consider Thy word in all my doings; yea, cause Thou me to gird the loins of my mind, that I be not deceived by mine own heart. For I know of men that speak Thy praises and give honour unto Thy Name with their lips, but they do that which is iniquitous. I know of heathen that greet one another in peace, but each man defileth his neighbour's wife privily. Yea, they bless one another in the gates, but when they be behind closed doors, they slander their brothers viciously. O Lord, I beseech Thee that Thou wouldest not suffer me to be like unto these men of two minds. O Lord, cause Thou me to be far from every worker of iniquity, for I know that secretly they long to devour me. Is it not also a light thing unto Thee to make a hedge round about me? Canst Thou speak but a word and cause mine enemies to flee from my presence? Assuredly Thou shalt protect me from mine adversaries which long to eat up mine inheritance. O God, I ask of Thee that Thou wouldest keep me in Thy sight at every moment. Turn not Thy face away from me, neither suffer Thou me to cease from abiding in Thy love.

"But Jesus said, Suffer little children,
and forbid them not, to come unto me:
for of such is the kingdom of heaven."

⁓⊙⊙⁓

MATTHEW 19:14 KJV

They Lie in Wait

O Lord, cause my loins to remain girded always. O God, cause also the light of my candle to shine continually. Lord, why should I depart from the hedge that Thou hast made round about me? What profit should I have, if I depart from Thy love? For can a lamb dwell safely in the field amongst the beasts? Or can a fish forsake the water, that it might dwell in a dry place? Therefore what fellowship doth a servant of Thine have with the wicked? For if I were to return unto the brethren that I forsook for the sake of righteousness, surely they would receive me speedily into their arms. Yea, they would take hold of me tightly; they would embrace me affectionately, that they might pierce me between my ribs, and cause my bowels to be spilled upon the ground. The lion doth long for a day in which he might sink his teeth into the gazelle that escaped his clutches aforetime. Mine enemies have reserved arrows and spears sharpened for my flesh. It is a foolish thing to depart from the protection of the Lord. They that turn aside are as fatted calves and aged wine prepared for a feast of gluttons. They shall be wholly eaten up by the wicked; yea, the earth shall not receive a drop of their blood. But the Lord shall not suffer me to depart from His presence. My God hath hidden me from the sight of all mine adversaries. I shall not be overcome by the lusts of this world, for the Lord hath filled me with His Spirit.

An Husband Unto Me

T he enemy encircled me; yea, the enemy encamped against my gates, but the Lord was an husband unto me. They fired arrows and brought swords thirsty for blood, but the Lord was an husband unto me. They intended to see me starve; they said amongst themselves that I would die of hunger, but the Lord was an husband unto me. They covered my wells; they cut down the fruitful trees that surround my city, but the Lord was an husband unto me. They pillaged the nations that were nigh unto me; they trode their feet upon the necks of the kings that dwelt nigh unto me, but the Lord was an husband unto me. They reasoned within their minds that my God would be silent as the gods of the nations that they previously conquered, but the Lord was an husband unto me. The Lord smote them, and confounded their plans, and caused them to fall upon their own swords because the Lord was an husband unto me. The Lord fed me and gave me drink because my God was an husband unto me. The Lord comforted me and gave rest unto my soul because the Lord was an husband unto me. Though I heard the cries of the heathen that lacked faith, there was peace in my house because the Lord was an husband unto me. I will live for ever and never taste death because the Lord is an husband unto me. I will rise up and praise Him with my entire being because the Lord is an husband unto me. I will be amongst the number of His saints when He cometh riding upon the clouds because Christ Jesus is an husband unto me.

TRUE RICHES

O Lord, I know that I shall not be moved, if I lean upon Thee. For Thou art the solid rock that causeth me to stand firmly; Thou art the strength in my knees and joints. Surely I will stand upright for all my days because I take joy in Thy precepts. O Lord, I have not desired to be praised by men; neither have I sought after earthly accolades. For what good can come from men praising my name? What doth it profit to let the praises of men fill my heart? I know that the man that blesseth me to my face can also curse me when I am far from him. I know that the companion of to day doth not always abide when the sun departeth. For this cause, I will not regard the vain words of men. Thou art my reward and my inheritance, O Lord. Wisdom is my recompense; knowledge and understanding are the finest fruits of my labour. O Lord, I long for Thy word far above any riches of the earth. For gold doth rust, and silver can be corrupted, but who can take the fear of God from my heart? Who can curse, whom Thou hast blessed? And who can bless, whom Thou hast cursed? My riches dwell safely within the storehouses of heaven. They shall not be depleted to day nor to morrow; yea, I shall have them perpetually. My riches shall follow me into life everlasting.

Desire Understanding

O how good it is to worship the Lord according to knowledge! O how commendable is the man that diligently seeketh after wisdom day and night! I will praise my God with understanding; I will lift my voice unto the God Who knoweth all things. I have sought His face amongst His creation; O Lord, reveal Thyself unto Thy elect. What man hast Thou rejected that sought Thee with his whole heart? Which servant of Thine didst Thou dismiss for supplicating unto Thee for understanding? When hast Thou ever disposed of a man that made Thy word his delight? From days of old, even unto this day, Thou dost always reward those that diligently seek after Thy face. I am not ashamed to say, Thou art my God. I am not ashamed to say, The wise of this world are foolish unto their own destruction. For one man saith, The sun ruleth over all things. Another sweareth his oaths by a detestable beast. Many there are that say, The creation created itself. Confounded and confused are they in life, and so shall they be in death, if they hearken not unto the cry of wisdom. But I will worship the Lord according to the knowledge that doth not perish. I will worship the Lord with my heart, with my mouth, and with my doings. I will learn of His ways and give myself unto the meditation of His word. I will bless His holy Name, for through His Spirit have I learned of salvation.

Exceeding Great Reward

As the gentle wind blew upon my face, I was reminded of Thee, O Lord. As I basked in the sun while he shined in his strength, I meditated pensively upon Thy word. As the trees swayed, and as the fowls chirped beautifully in my ears, I imagined the praises before Thy heavenly throne. O Lord, see to it that I praise Thee in Thy presence for evermore. For Thou hast been ever present in my thoughts and my desires. When I sought Thee, behold, Thou wast before my face and I knew it not. Thou art God, and it is in Thy power to seal the wisdom that Thou hast put within me. It is in Thy power to see that I turn neither left nor right from that which is just and true. For what profit can I hope to gain, if I separate myself from Thy perfect will for my life? If I were to forsake Thee by returning unto the sins that I cast behind me, surely I would be digging my own pit, and surely I would be falling into my own snare. But Thou wilt not suffer me to fall from Thy grace. If I stumble, it is to the end that I might learn to walk before Thee perfectly. If I remember Thee, surely Thou wilt remember me. If I do that which Thou desirest, surely I shall receive of Thee that which I desire. For Thou art a God of great generosity; Thou art a rewarder of those that diligently seek after Thy face. O Lord, Thou art my exceeding great reward.

The Death of Former Things

I will not look back; nay, my portion will not be that of Lot's wife. I will not covet that which I put away for the sake of righteousness. My heart shall not desire nor think upon the lusts of my youth. For what good doth it serve to imagine former revellings? What doth it profit to think upon the taste of strong drink after having tasted the heavenly gift and the good word of God? Should I willingly place my feet within a snare for a second time? Should I trip over a stumblingblock that hath already been leapt over? For when I moved about in my own will and after my own flesh, I desired and could not obtain, I lusted and had not; and though I asked for blessings of God, He granted them not because of my foul intentions. Though I have given up that which I was once enamoured with, and though my flesh hath been put to death, truly I live for evermore in Christ. Truly I now possess far greater riches than that which I cast away as dung. I will cut off from my life those who seek to tempt me to sin; I will remove from my sight every worker of iniquity. I will not know a blasphemer nor a child of Belial. My companion shall be my brother; yea, my counsellor shall be a man that speaketh in accordance to the oracles of God. I will walk joyfully toward the light of my salvation which hath also been a lamp unto my feet.

Thou Art My Rest

O Lord, my hands are blistered, and my knees are exceedingly weary. My eyes are like unto boulders in weight, and my throat is like unto salt in dryness. From heavy labour and tiresome work, my soul doth faint within me. O Lord, when shall I receive rest from this life of toil and heavy burdens? For there is no place of rest for my senses. When I lift up mine eyes from staring at the ground, behold, there walketh a woman in harlot's attire. O Lord, mine ears have been defiled by the perverse words that my neighbours speak in my hearing. O Lord, when I walk about the market, my nose doth smell the incense which the heathen burn unto their idols. Whither can I go, and to what place can I flee? Where can I hide to escape the oppression? Selah. The Lord hath commanded me to abide in my prayer closet: the Lord hath led me to a place of solitude. The Lord hath shewed me a secret place of comfort under the shadow of the Almighty. Though I be amongst a people that mock His holy word, and though I be amongst a nation that hath forsaken the God of Israel, the Lord hath not left me alone in this grievous land. The Lord doth walk with me and doth guide me by His right hand. As a man doth lead his camel to a well, that its thirst may be quenched, so hath the Lord dealt with me. He hath been unto me a little sanctuary in the place of my sojourning. He hath promised me that I shall receive eternal rest for my soul. O Lord, Thou art my rest; O Lord, Thou art my Comforter.

Be Thou Moved by the Spirit

Let the Spirit of the most High God dwell between thy shoulders; be thou moved by the everlasting Spirit. For whither He shall lead thee, there thou shalt prosper; and the words which He shall speak unto thee, they shall surely bring thee life. The evildoers shall be utterly destroyed; every one that chooseth darkness over light shall bear his iniquity. Their blood is upon their own heads, for they trust in that which doth rust and that which hath no power to save. But the righteous are not so, for they trust in the God of Israel. A righteous man, though he fall, shall surely be lifted up; even by the hairs of his head shall he be lifted up by the Spirit of the Lord. Selah. O Lord, blot not my name out of Thy book. O Lord, remember me not according to the evil which I wrought in mine ignorance. For the burden of mine iniquity is far too heavy to bear upon mine own shoulders. If I have no redemption in Thee, O Jesus, who then shall deliver me from my sins? If I be not bought with Thy blood, or if Thy sacrifice appertaineth not unto me, how then shall I stand on the day when I am judged? O Lord, flee not from my midst, neither suffer Thou me to depart from Thy presence. For without Thee, I shall succumb to the sin which doth bind all men that perish. Without Thee, I shall die the death that bringeth dishonour and shame. But Thou wilt shew Thyself merciful and exceedingly pitiful; Thou wilt not suffer me to perish, for I have put my trust in Thee. Thou shalt dwell in Thy temple, for it hath been sanctified and hallowed. The glory of the Lord shall appear before mine eye, and I shall shout, and fall upon my face and worship.

His Temple

I will offer the sacrifice of thanksgiving unto the Lord with the fruit of my lips. Upon the altar of incense before His heavenly throne hath my prayer been placed; O Lord, let it be a sweet smelling savour unto Thee. O my God, I have eaten of Thy table; the bread which is before Thee hath been ever so delightful unto me. Thou hast washed me, O Lord; Thou hast sprinkled me with that which is holier than the water of separation. From between the Cherubim, Thou hast spoken unto me; who am I, that I should go beyond the veil? Who am I, that I should behold Thy face? For the sacrifice which I placed upon Thy altar was not the fat of bullocks nor the fat of goats. I confessed my sins unto Thee with a broken and contrite heart and Thou didst receive me. Truly Thou hast lit Thy candlestick within my heart. Wisdom and understanding have I received of Thee because I feared my God. I have faith in the knowledge of Thy word which hath been greater unto me than a thousand counsellors. By Thy strength and by Thy might, I have overcome and endured. And because I have received Thy Holy Spirit, I know that I am Thine eternally. For this cause shall I present myself as a living sacrifice unto the Lord. He hath taken away my imperfections; He hath clothed me with immortality; the Lord hath caused me to remain in His temple for evermore.

Who Am I?

Who am I, O Lord? Who am I, that Thou wouldest think to shine Thy face upon me? What uprightness hast Thou found in my heart? Yea, have I been without sin since the time of my birth? For assuredly I know that it is not for my righteousness that Thou hast gifted me with Thy grace. For if I were to say that I am deserving of the great gift that Thou hast so mercifully given unto me, I would be speaking in deceit. If I were to boast that I obtained wealth by my own hands and by my own cunning, I would be speaking as a son of Belial. For all blessings come from heaven, and all riches belong unto the God of glory. Who am I, that I should be a partaker of Thy goodness? Who am I, that I should be seated at the table of the Lord? Verily Thy lovingkindness hath been shewed forth through the multitude of mercies which Thou hast shewed unto me. O Lord, put a song in my heart, that I may sing unto Thee. Cause my voice to be lifted, and to be heard by men, to the end that they might praise Thee in unity with me. For I desire to do Thy will, O Lord; I desire to see Thy face, O God. My entire being is satiated by Thy Holy Spirit.

"The steps of a good man are ordered by the Lord: and he delighteth in his way."

❧

PSALM 37:23 KJV

A Poem for Communion

How goodly it is to rejoice with our loins girded. Truly it is comely to be circumspect and to examine the inner man. O how I have longed for the bread of life. O how I have longed to drink this cup with Thee, my God. For truly Thou hast saved us, O Lord. There was no place too distant or obscure, there was no hole nor crevice in which Thou didst not search for Thy lost sheep. Selah. I rejoice with Thee, my King. Thou hast put a staff in my hand and a song in my mouth, that I might worship Thee. Blessing and honour, glory and power be unto the Lamb. For Thou hast turned bitterness into joy and sadness into mirth, and now I will sup with Thee for evermore. Selah. The sun gave his light to shew forth Thy glory; the moon gave a marvellous sign in reverence of the bridegroom. My chief joy is the new Jerusalem which cometh down from heaven. For within this city, there reigneth a King; and within this city, there standeth a temple; and in that place shall I worship for evermore.

Sing Unto the Lord

The Lord of hosts, He reigneth for ever! The Lord Almighty, He doth rest His feet in Zion! Thou art the King of glory, O God; Thou art the ruler of the nations and the judge of all creation. Beautiful is Thy throne, O Lord! Excellent is Thy sceptre, O King! Whosoever refuseth to do obeisance unto Thee, even that very soul shall be slaughtered and struck down before Thy face. O Lord, all things have been put under Thy feet; all creation must submit unto Thee! Speak but a word, O God: give Thy commandment and the desolate land of Israel shall become like unto the garden of Eden. Thy Name is one, O Lord! Living waters hast Thou poured out in Jerusalem, that they may bring healing unto the sick, and that all they which do thirst after life may be quenched. Thou art righteous, Thou art just, Thou art holy, and Thou art highly exalted! Sing unto the Lord, all ye subjects of the king! Sing unto the Lord, ye friends of God!

A Poem of Repentance

O Lord, O Lord, I have sinned, I have sinned. Before the face of God and before the faces of men have I sinned. As the stiffnecked fathers of old, I closed my ears to the wise counsel and forewarning of the Lord. Though I knew the manner in which a servant of Thine ought to conduct himself, I sinned nonetheless in my folly. Like unto the hypocrites, I ate and drank with mockers and scorners. With my mouth I blessed Thy holy Name while in my bedchamber, and with my mouth I spake idle words while amongst the heathen. I have been of a double mind; yea, my conversation was not chaste. Therefore my nakedness was exposed, and Thou didst suffer me to be put to shame openly. But Thou, O Lord, art just and righteous. Thou, O Lord, art merciful and longsuffering. Thou hast brought my sin to light to the end that I might repent. O my God, remove not Thy quickening Spirit nor Thy precious word from my heart. For I am broken and contrite, and Thou hast humbled me thoroughly. Teach me Thy way, that I may walk therein; cause Thou me to lead sinners unto repentance and immersion. For Thou art worthy to be praised in the city and in the field; Thou art worthy to be praised openly in the gates, and Thou art worthy to be praised when no man seeth. Yea, Thou art worthy to be praised at every hour of the day. For though it be during the reign of the sun, or though it be during the dominion of the moon, Thy holy Name shall be worshipped and praised.

BREACHES IN MINE ARMOUR

O Lord, how admonishing are Thy rebukes! O Lord, how edifying are Thy teachings! For when Thou shewest me the errors of my ways, and when Thou revealest breaches in mine armour, it is to the end that I might be perfect and blameless in Thy sight. O God, if Thou wouldest have withheld Thy chastisement from me, I would be altogether reprobate. If Thou wouldest have held Thy peace when I sinned in mine ignorance, I would have died in my folly. But Thou hast shewed me Thy love, in that Thou didst not suffer me to remain in transgression. Thou hast shewed me mercy, in that Thou didst not spare Thy rod from beating on my sides. O Lord, Thou art a Father unto me, in that Thou sufferest me not to sin to my own detriment. For if I were to transgress, would it not be to my own harm? If I were to forsake Thy commandment, would I not be falling upon mine own sword? O Lord, it is better to be rebuked of Thee unto repentance, than to fall from Thy grace for cleaving unto iniquity. O Lord, it is better for a man to humble himself in Thy sight, than for him to be abased before the faces of men. O God, cease not from correcting my shortcomings. If Thou see a spot in my garment, or a blemish in my heart, cleanse Thou me with Thy perfect word. O Lord, I pray that Thou wouldest never cease from speaking unto me by Thy perfect Spirit.

Fall Short in Comparison

O Lord, Thou hast made man in the image of God: after the likeness of the Almighty hast Thou created mankind. That which a man doth possess naturally to understand, and to know, and to acquire wisdom cometh from the Lord, and doth fall short in comparison to that which appertaineth unto the Lord. For a man doth see with his eyes that which is before him, but the sight of the Lord is greater, in that He looketh down from the highest heaven. As the eagle soareth high and looketh down upon the earth, so doth the Lord see the works of every man, and He doth judge them accordingly. A man doth hear with his ears the voice of his neighbour, and the sound of a falling tree, and the howl of his dog, but the Lord heareth the cry of blood spilled upon the ground in murder. The Lord doth hear the prayers of His saints; and the Lord doth hear every idle word that men speak with their lips. A man can discern a fire by the smell of smoke in his nostrils, but the Lord smelleth the sins of a wicked man, for they are a loathsome stench unto the Highest. With their hands, men make vessels, and houses, and weapons, and books; but the Lord, with His hands, created the heavens and the earth and all that is within them. O Lord, how excellent is all that Thou art! For man doth fall short in comparison to Thy majesty. As a leaf is to the forest, or as a raindrop is to the sea, so doth man fall short in comparison to Thee! As a blade of grass is to the open field, or as a grain of sand is to the shore, so doth man fall short in comparison to Thee! How worthy of praise by all men is Thy holy Name! How excellent is all that Thou art, O Lord!

SIMILITUDES

U nto what shall I liken the excellent word of the Lord? And in what similitude shall His word be known? For it is as milk to the sucking babe; to those that are fully grown, it is as the finest of bread. When men take good heed to obey the word of God, it is as a lantern held in the right hand of a traveller walking on a dark path. Seest thou a seed? Is not the word of the Lord observed in it? For as a seed is sown into the ground and groweth through water and sunlight, so doth the word of God grow within men that are filled with the Holy Spirit and that keep His commandments. To those that despise His commandments and forsake His judgements, His word is a consuming fire. As a rod doth beat upon the sides of a disobedient child, so doth the word of the Lord discipline them which He calleth sons. Have we not all father and mother? Have our elders not bestowed wisdom upon us through their instruction? The word of the Lord is a father to even an orphan. And to those whose mothers died during the travail of childbirth, is not His wisdom as one that giveth suck? Look upon the seas; behold the great deep. Is not the word of the Lord seen in it? For as the surface of the sea is beheld but the depths are unaccountable, so doth men comprehend some principles of doctrine, but the mysteries of the word of God are innumerable. All creation doth bear witness; even the host of heaven testify of His greatness. Why then, O brutish man, dost thou harden thy heart and deny that which is so clearly seen?

THE BEAUTY OF THE LORD

Beauty and magnificence belong unto the Lord God. Who can describe the great comeliness of the Lord? He that hath commanded the sun to give his light, shall He not shine much brighter? With a word, He spake it that the grass of the earth should be green; He chooseth also the colour of the sky: be thou blue. Nay, be thou red. The same God hath also arrayed the lilies of the field with a marvellous visage. Who then can fathom the hem of His garment? Out of His mouth proceedeth a fire capable of consuming the heavens and the earth. His eyes are ten thousand times brighter than the sun. How dreadful, how terrible, how wonderful might His face be like? His hands have made and fashioned the sardius stone, topaz, diamond, beryl, and every other precious stone of the earth. How much greater is the beauty of His throne? Though a man be rich in gold and silver, can any account for the riches within the storehouses of heaven? The temple made with hands was exceedingly magnificent; yea, the house of the Lord was admired of all nations. How much more the new Jerusalem which cometh down from heaven? Though He came unto His own with no form nor comeliness, the day draweth nigh when He shall appear with glory in the clouds. Though He was in the world and the world knew Him not, upon His appearing, every eye shall see Him and marvel. Yea, every knee shall also bow, and every tongue shall openly confess that Jesus Christ is Lord.

THY RIGHTEOUSNESS SHALL ABIDE

Blessed art Thou, Lord God Almighty; holy, holy, holy is the Lord God! Thou art the mighty God of Israel. He Who Was, He Who Is, and He Who Is To Come; Thou art the Eternal One. For Thou hast overcome and defeated sin and death; Thou hast wholly destroyed Thine enemies; Thou hast trampled upon the dragon and the venomous serpent; Thou hast utterly consumed the heathen as stubble by the word of Thy mouth. Thou hast judged righteously and no iniquity can be found in Thee. Thou didst not respect the persons of the rich, neither didst Thou scoff at the poor of the earth. But Thou hast righteously given unto every man the recompense of his doings. O that men would live according to Thy ways! O that men would praise Thee! For surely they would then be spared from perishing. Thou hast warned, Thou hast been longsuffering, Thou hast been merciful and very gracious, but men have despised Thy Name. I will not be counted amongst the number of those that transgress. I will not share the portion of them that go down into the pit. I will rise up and bless Thy holy Name, O Lord. Go thy way, O man. Go thy way, thou righteous man: thou shalt inherit life for evermore. Go thy way, thou wicked man that dost work iniquity: thy worm shall not die, neither shall thy fire be quenched perpetually. But the righteousness of the Lord shall abide for ever and ever.

Rebuke the Thick Cloud

I poured out my complaint unto the Almighty: O Lord, when wilt Thou visit me? For my laughter hath been changed into weeping, and my countenance is like unto sackcloth. I sprinkled ashes upon my head and cried bitterly in my bedchamber: Save me, O Lord! For Thou art my hope; Thou alone art my Saviour; Thou shalt uplift me when I have fallen abruptly. Though I make my bed amongst the dust of the ground, surely at the sound of Thy trumpet shall I arise with joy. Surely Thou shalt rebuke the thick cloud of darkness that hath pursued hard after me. For Thou art the light of the dawn; Thou art the bright and morning star which hath illuminated my path. I know that Thou shalt save me from dismay and sorrow. Thy word shall bring joy unto my heart eternally.

A Poem of Healing

O Lord God, remember me: remember even Thy servant Jonathan. Incline thine ear unto the voice of my weeping, O Lord; hear thou my prayer, and answer me speedily. For I am sore afflicted in my body, and pain hath consumed me from the crown of my head to the soles of my feet. Sleep hath also departed from mine eyes; my nights have been full of tossings to and fro. Whither shall I flee to escape the infirmity that doth cripple me? Where shall I find a remedy for my soul? O Lord, remember me not according to the evil which I wrought in days past; remember me not according to the lasciviousness of my youth. For in former days, I walked about as one that hateth instruction and understanding. In the days before I knew Thee, I moved about as mine own master. For this cause, I had no means of defence against the wiles of the enemy. Therefore as a drunken man that refuseth to forsake his wine, I blindly stumbled into the snare that he laid for me. Though Thou didst forewarn me of the danger that cometh from rebellion, I considered not Thy reproof, for I knew not Thy voice. Though Thou didst shout and cry unto me, I hearkened not unto Thy call as one that considereth not the sound of the wind blowing. And because of mine iniquity, I was viciously attacked by the ravenous lion as a sheep that hath wandered far from the flock. Then did I shout, and then did I cry; and though Thou couldest have left me to be devoured, Thy staff smote the wild beast, and thou didst carry me on Thy shoulders to a place of safety. O how excellent is Thy lovingkindness toward the sons of men! O Lord, I know that Thou art a healing God: therefore bless Thou my bread, and bless Thou my water. Quicken me according to Thy infinite mercies, and according to Thy excellent word. For now I know the voice of my Shepherd; now I will move about in fear of my Master for all the days of my life. It is my good pleasure to do that which is wellpleasing in Thy sight. Whereas I before pleased my own flesh and fulfilled the desires of mine own mind, I will now fulfil that which Thou hast created me to do. I will fear my God, and give glory unto His Name: for His will for my life is perfect.

"And even to your old age I am he;
and even to hoar hairs will I carry you:
I have made, and I will bear;
even I will carry, and will deliver you."

ᏮᎧᏯ

Isaiah 46:4 KJV

He Shall Gather

Look down, O Lord: look down upon the children of men. Many there are that have forsaken Thee; many there are that have forgotten Thy holy Name; many there are that practice the evil imaginations of their hearts, but the Lord hath left a remnant. There be a few that have remained faithful. There are a number, which Thou knowest, of Thy saints with uplifted arms at every moment. Throughout the four corners of the earth, there are those who lift their voices in honour of the mighty God continually. I know for certain that there be those who pray without ceasing. My God hath shewed me that there be some who have not fornicated with idols. Though I behold them not with mine eyes, my spirit doth testify that I have brethren in every nation. There remain priests and kings fit to reign upon the earth. The Lord hath placed righteous men in every office of His church. Selah. Judge not after the sight of thine eyes; neither conclude thou a matter based upon thine own understanding. Consider the view of the Lord and thou shalt not err. Remain in the Spirit and thou shalt not be alone. Seek the Lord with thy whole heart and He shall gather thee unto thy brethren in due season.

We Thy People

O Lord God, Thou couldest have held Thy peace; yea, Thou couldest have left man alone to his devices, but Thou didst speak into his heart instead. My God, Thou art truly good and righteous, for no man can say that Thou art silent. Thou spakest through thy prophets and through the wise men of old and now have we received Thy word through Thy beloved Son, Jesus Christ. When the brethren are gathered together, and when our voices are lifted in unity, Thy Spirit doth move amongst us abundantly. And when a brother or sister hath fallen ill, or when trouble and anguish hath taken hold of them, Thou dost always move Thy people to comfort them that are in need. And through the laying on of hands, and through the mouths of Thy saints, truly Thou dost heal Thy people. O Lord God, we Thy people love Thee eternally.

Thy Church

C ome hither, my brother: put thine hand in mine, and worship the Lord with me. That which thou hast hath been given thee by God, it is very precious indeed. That which I have received of the Lord give I thee, for all is common among brethren of the same house. For my tears were not by their lonesome: thine eyes too shed tears when I was in dismay. Thy laughter found a companion in me, for thy joy did I share when thou didst receive that which we had prayed for. Verily, verily, I see Christ Jesus in thee. Verily, verily, His light doth shine through thee onto me. The Lord doth take pleasure in the unity of His saints. The Lord doth dwell amongst those that love one another as He loved them. I thank Thee, O Lord, for Thou hast not left me alone at any moment. I am surrounded by Thy love when I am surrounded by Thy church.

Praise with Thy Entire Being

The heavens and the earth belong unto the Lord God. The breath in thy nostrils, and the members of thy body, they too belong unto the Lord God. Why dost thou praise Him with only thy mouth? Clap thy hands, O man; stomp thy feet, thou son of Adam. For if thou neglect, the very stones shall surpass thee in praise. Give therefore all thy soul unto Him; praise with all thy strength and might, and give thy life unto Him. Let it not be spoken, yea, let it not be uttered that thou withheldest thy praise from Him. If there be breath in thy nostrils, and if there be life in thy body, praise the Lord with all that thou hast. O man, even if thou art feeble, and even if thou art sickly, praise the Lord, for He hath the power to make thee whole. Praise thou not as the hypocrites do. For they sing at the highest notes; yea, they dance vigorously with their bodies, but all the while they praise, they have murder and adultery in their hearts. Let it not be spoken that thy praise was in vain. Praise the Lord; for the enemy shall be smitten at the sound of thy worship. Praise the Lord; for the bands of sickness shall be loosed from thee by the giver of thy joy. Praise the Lord; and see that thou do so with thy entire being.

Prayer of the Youthful Servant

O most High God, Thou that didst create the heavens and the earth by the word of Thy mouth. Thou that didst in the days of old declare Thy Name through miraculous signs and wonders which no man can refute. Thou that didst cause righteous men to be exalted; and Thou that didst cause wicked men to be destroyed. O most High, hearken unto the prayer of Thy youthful servant. For I am but a child before Thee; I am but a grasshopper in Thy sight; nay, I am but a grain of dust under Thy sandal. Who can save my soul from the snare of the enemy but Thy Son? Who can deliver me from the way of sin but Thy Spirit? Hear me, O most High, for I am compassed about by iniquity; I am as a city attacked on every side. Whither can I flee to escape the weakness of my flesh and the lusts of my body? For how can I say unto mine eyes, Desire not? And how can I say unto my mind, Think not? What strength of my own do I have to forsake the sin which doth cripple me? O most High, Thou knowest that I have not walked before Thee perfectly, but Thou art able to blot out my transgressions. Thou art able to cause my flesh to die; yea, Thou art able to transform that which was shapen in iniquity. O most High God, wash me thoroughly with Thy clean water and cleanse me with the sprinkling of Thy blood. I beseech Thee that Thou wouldest change the desires of my heart and the desires of my body, that they might be conformed unto Thy perfect will. Utterly destroy, I pray Thee, the sin which hath besieged and compassed me about. For Thou art the most High God, the God of hosts; who can stand against Thee? What man can lift his fist toward Thee without it consuming away before his eyes? What beast can snarl and shew his teeth unto Thee without Thy indignation being poured out upon him? What unclean spirit can withstand the word of Thy mouth? O most High, save me, that I sin not against Thee in word or in deed. Save me, that I sin not against Thee with my mind or with mine eyes.

BE THOU WITH ME

O most High, how can a man perfect his ways without Thy word of truth? How can a man forsake the folly of his flesh without Thy Spirit to instruct him of righteousness? Through the scriptures of old, Thou hast given me joy; I give reverence and honour unto my God, for through His law have I been admonished. They that walk without Thy word tread upon a path of darkness, but I have found a lamp unto my feet in Thy holy scriptures. Selah. Even as Thou wast with the great patriarchs and the prophets of old, be Thou with me. For when Thou didst walk with Thy beloved Abraham, his faith was accounted unto him for righteousness. Give this faith unto me, O Lord. When Isaac was bound upon the altar, he murmured no complaint, neither did he seek to save his own life; and because of his willingness to be a sacrifice unto Thee, he was delivered from death by the Angel of the Lord. Heavenly Father God, suffer me to love not my own life unto death as Thy servant Isaac. As Thou wast with holy Israel, be Thou even with me. For when Jacob feared that his brother would smite him along with his wives and children, he supplicated unto Thee and Thou didst deliver him from the hand of Esau. O Lord, deliver me from mine enemies even as Thou didst unto father Jacob. As Thou wast with Moses, be Thou with me, O God. For through Thy Spirit, Moses was faithful in all Thy house; and through Thy Spirit, he was the meekest man upon the face of the earth. Though he was of a slow tongue, and though he possessed no eloquence of speech, Thou didst put Thy word within his mouth and made him to shout, Hear, O Israel. I know that my God is the same yesterday, to day and for evermore. I know that the Spirit which wrought great works through the holy men of old can do the same through me though I be but a feeble man. I will therefore prostrate myself before my God and believe in His holy Name. And as He was with the fathers of old, so shall He be with me.

Love Even Thine Enemies

O Jesus, when Thou saidst unto me that I should love even mine enemies, my heart thought to rebel. How, Lord, thought I, shall I do good unto men that have only done me harm? How, O Lord, shall I take that which Thou hast given me and put it into the bosoms of men when they have only beaten and robbed me at every hour? But in my moment of rebellion, I heard Thee say unto me, Thinkest thou that men have robbed thee? When thou gavest unto him that was in need, verily thou gave it unto Me. And when thou receivedst nothing of him in return, did not I reward thee greatly? Why sayest thou then that thou hast been robbed? Or when thou saidest that men have beaten thee and done thee harm, verily it was Me that they smote. Why sayest thou then that thou hast been beaten? For no alms shall ever go unnoticed, and no good deed shall ever go unrewarded. O Lord, Thou dost always speak well in Thy sayings, and Thou dost always judge righteously. I shall obey Thee in every thing, and in every thing shall I give Thee thanks.

Get Thee Behind Me, O Satan

Comest thou against the most High God, O Satan? Whom dost thou make thy boast against? Yea, whom dost thou array thy soldiers to war against? Deceive not thyself in thinking that thou hast spoken against me by thy false accusations; nay, thou hast not come out to battle against me, but thou hast defied the living God Whom I serve. Knowest thou not, O Satan, that I am covered by the blood of the Lamb? Knowest thou not, O Devil, that thou hast no power over the people of God? Thou must therefore get behind me, O Satan; the Lord rebuke thee! For thou hast no place in the temple of God, and thy desire to devour his sheep shall not be accomplished. For how canst thou murder, whom God hath given everlasting life? How canst thou steal that which I have stored in heaven? O Satan, thou art for ever subdued through the Name of Jesus Christ; yea, thou art for ever beneath my feet, for the God of heaven hath put thee there. O fallen one, thy sins shall not be forgiven thee; neither shalt thou receive atonement for thine iniquities. For Thy everlasting portion is with thine angels, and with thy children in the lake which burneth with fire and brimstone. O Devil, canst thou tell that thou dost labour in vain to deceive me? Canst thou tell that thou art but a dead man? Get thee therefore behind me, O Satan! For thou shalt never receive my worship nor my praise. Get thee behind me, O Devil! Thou shalt never ascend unto the throne of the Lord. Get thee behind me, O Satan! Thou art cursed for ever.

All Things Are Possible for God

O Lord, what can men utter that would sufficiently declare Thy greatness? For Thy power hath no bounds; neither can the heavens nor the earth contain Thy excellency. For how can the Creator of all things be limited to the understanding of men? How can Thy hand be shortened, if by it all things were made? Truly nothing is impossible for my God. For men doubted that the fountains of the great deep would ever be broken up, yet they drowned in their sins. Pharaoh saw Israel encamped by the sea, and reasoned within his heart that the wilderness had shut them up. Did not that same sea drown the horse and the rider along with the chariot of Pharaoh while Israel walked through it dryshod? The men of Jericho trusted in their wall; but the Lord, at the sound of a great shout, smote it, that it fell down flat. The giant cursed David by his gods, yet his head was cut off his shoulders by a mere youth. Truly nothing is impossible for my God. Hath He not given sight unto the blind? Hath His word not caused the deaf to receive their hearing? Did not Lazarus and the daughter of Jairus flee from the grave upon hearing the commandment of God? Why then should I doubt that He will also raise me from the dead at the sound of the last trump? I know that all things are possible for my God. I know that He is mighty to save in the day of my trouble.

FAITH

T hough there be limits and impossibilities with men, the Lord God hath power to do whatsoever pleaseth Him. The man that believeth on the Name of God, the same can achieve all things through faith in the Lord God. For mountains have been removed, and seas have been parted by men that called upon the Name of the Lord in faith. Battles against mighty foes have been won by the stretching forth of faithful hands unto the most High God. Prisoners have been unshackled, and bars have been broken by supplication made unto the God of hosts. Whoremongers have forsaken their ways, and harlots have repented of their sins upon hearing the word of faith in their ears. Men that aforetime bowed unto wood, stone, and metals laid with vermilion have burned their idols into ashes upon seeing the power of the Name of Jesus Christ. The dead have forsaken the grave: many that had given up the ghost were quickened by prayer made unto the God that liveth for ever. Men that were feeble, yea, men that were lightly esteemed have been exalted unto everlasting honour for submitting themselves unto the will of the Lord. Women that were mocked for being childless among their peers gave birth unto great prophets: for they first shewed themselves faithful, and then they conceived. Sight hath been given unto the blind: though they saw not with their eyes, they believed that God had power to heal. And after sight had been given them in the spirit, their eyes were also opened in the flesh, for their faith made them whole. The deaf have been given their hearing: though they heard not the voices of men, the voice of the Lord was manifested first in their hearts. And because they hearkened unto the word of God in their minds, they also received hearing in their bodily ears: for they deemed that which is heard in the spirit to be greater than that which is heard in the flesh. Many miracles, great signs and wonders have been wrought by the God of eternity. Since the days of Adam, there hath not been one man that was forsaken when he called upon the Name of the Lord in faith. Faith is stronger than sin; faith is mightier than death. The grave hath no power over those that hope in the Lord. Though the nations of the earth be gathered together to slay a man of God, the Word of the Lord shall consume them as stubble by the fire of His mouth.

Hallelujah! Thank God.

"Let every thing that hath breath praise the LORD.
Praise ye the LORD."

ᴄᲊᏰᲒᏰᏰ

PSALM 150:6 KJV